Sponsoring Change

A Guide to the Governance Aspects of Project Sponsorship

APM SIG GUIDE SERIES

Directing Change: A Guide to Governance of Project Management
ISBN: 978-1-903494-15-8

Co-Directing Change: A Guide to the Governance of Multi-Owned Projects
ISBN: 978-1-903494-94-3

Models to Improve the Management of Projects
ISBN: 978-1-903494-80-6

APM Introduction to Programme Management
ISBN: 978-1-903494-63-9

Interfacing Risk and Earned Value Management
ISBN: 978-1-903494-24-0

Prioritising Project Risks
ISBN: 978-1-903494-27-1

Earned Value Management
ISBN: 978-1-903494-26-4

Introduction to Project Planning
ISBN: 978-1-903494-28-8

Sponsoring Change

A Guide to the Governance Aspects of Project Sponsorship

APM Governance of Project Management Specific Interest Group

Association for Project Management

Association for Project Management
Ibis House, Regent Park
Summerleys Road, Princes Risborough
Buckinghamshire
HP27 9LE

British Library Cataloguing in Publication Data is available
ISBN 10: 1-903494-30-1
ISBN 13: 978-1-903494-30-1

Cover design by Fountainhead Creative Consultants
Typeset by RefineCatch Ltd, Bungay, Suffolk
Copyedited by Dorothy Courtis
Printed by Latimer Trend and Company

Contents

List of figures   vi

Foreword   vii

Acknowledgements   viii

1   Purpose   1

2   Why every project needs a sponsor   2

3   Organisational context   3

4   The attributes for successful sponsorship   4

5   What the sponsor does for the board   6

6   What the sponsor does for the project manager   8

7   What the sponsor does for other stakeholders   10

Conclusion   12

Appendix 1 – Special cases of organisational context   13

Appendix 2 – Choosing a project sponsor   17

Appendix 3 – Sponsorship checklists   18

Appendix 4 – Legal aspects   22

Appendix 5 – Bibliography   23

List of figures

3.1   Organisational context   3

A.1   Programme and project sponsorship   14

A.2   Multi-organisational projects   15

A.3   Different roles   16

Foreword

Project sponsors create or destroy value. Their role determines whether or not each project gets off to a good start, continues throughout the project and outlasts that of the project manager. Sponsors link corporate direction and accountability with programmes and projects. They transmit information and decisions downward to the project, represent the project upwards, communicate with stakeholders, care for the project context and are accountable for project benefits. Hence this role is pivotal in the governance of project management and the broader ongoing success of organisations.

The eleven key questions related to project sponsorship given in the publication *Directing Change* published by the Association for Project Management remain valid. However it has been observed that the sponsor role is still widely misunderstood and poorly practised. Hence the need for this further more specific guidance.

The guide explains the rationale for the sponsorship role, clarifies the range of governance related duties and provides concise practical aids.

As with the two previous successful publications from the same study group, *Directing Change* and *Co-Directing Change,* it applies to all types of organisation and across sectors. We believe its use will improve governance, bringing greater rewards to organisations undertaking significant projects as well as to their owners and to wider stakeholders.

We commend its adoption.

Bob Assirati
Major Projects Director, OGC
(Office of Government Commerce)

Mike Nichols
Chairman, APM

Acknowledgements

This document was prepared by the Governance of Project Management Specific Interest Group of the Association for Project Management between July 2008 and July 2009.

The editing committee listed below would welcome any feedback:

Martin Hopkinson	mhopkinson@qinetiq.com
Ian Isaac	ian.isaac@o2.com
Peter Parkes	peter.parkes@peakperformance.gb.com
David Shannon	David.Shannon@opmg.co.uk

Other members of the group who made a significant contribution are:

John Bolton, David Bright, John Caton, Suzanne Davison, Peter Deary, Miles Dixon, Keith Gray, Peter Gulliver, Michael Hougham, Ole Jonny Klakegg, Carol A Long, Hartley Millar, Amerjit Walia, Brian Wernham, Charles Willbe.

The authors wish to express their thanks to all who contributed to the development of these guidelines and to the peer reviewers whose valuable feedback on the final draft resulted in several improvements.

1 Purpose

The purpose of this guide is to influence directors and senior managers to adopt excellent practices regarding project sponsorship. It does not replace existing texts and methodologies on sponsorship, but rather focuses on the governance aspects of the role.

It explains:
- why every project needs a sponsor,
- the attributes of sponsorship that are critical to success and
- what a sponsor does.

Project sponsors are variously titled, for example senior responsible owner or group manager, according to practice within their organisations. They may also be located at different levels in their organisation. An organisation may prioritise the attributes of sponsors differently dependent on whether a project is internal or external, or if they are the client or contracting organisation.

Help is given in choosing and appointing suitable sponsors (Appendix 2).

The guide also helps existing and aspiring project sponsors to:
- fulfil governance requirements of the board (Appendix 3),
- comply with legal requirements (Appendix 4),
- understand the role and
- develop their competence.

Projects, programmes, project management and programme management are defined in the *APM Body of Knowledge*, the *PMBOK*, *BS6079*, and the UK Office of Government Commerce's guide *Managing Successful Programmes*. For brevity, this guide uses the term 'project' as being inclusive of project based programmes. Thus, when this guide recommends that every project should have a sponsor, it implies, equally, that every programme should have a sponsor.

Our use of the term "board" applies to executive boards, their equivalents in the public sector and to councils in companies limited by guarantee. It does not mean project boards, which are described separately under the section on organisational context.

2 Why every project needs a sponsor

Separation of decision-making responsibilities

Whilst a project manager may contribute towards all project-related decisions, for reasons of sound governance, there are some decisions that they should not be authorised to take. These decisions include:
- the purpose of the project,
- the project objectives,
- the top-level contingency provisions,
- the project's priority relative to other projects owned by the organisation,
- who is appointed to the position of project manager or whether they should continue in the role,
- the deployment of resources not managed directly by the project manager and
- whether or not the project should be started, proceed to the next stage or be discontinued.

Such decisions are important, require clarity and are often interrelated. Hence it is good practice that they should be communicated to the project manager and agreed with them via one key role; the project sponsor.

Accountability for the realisation of benefits

Project benefits are often realised outside the project manager's domain and sometimes years after their role has ceased to exist. The sponsor, with a wider remit within the organisation, is therefore required to ensure that mechanisms are in place for the realisation of benefits.

Oversight of the project management function

It is sometimes appropriate to challenge the information and forecasts produced by the project manager. By applying consistent oversight, expertise and sound judgement, the sponsor should be in a position to do so either themselves or by seeking independent verification.

Stakeholder management

Project strategy often requires that stakeholders be engaged at a more senior level than the project manager. Stakeholder identification and stakeholder communications policy should be overseen by the project sponsor, thus clarifying stakeholder management responsibilities.

3 Organisational context

Project sponsorship is a critical component in an organisation's governance of project management. Figure 3.1 shows the links that the sponsor has with other key parties.

The organisation may own a portfolio of programmes and projects. In such a portfolio there is a need for the relationship between sponsors to be clearly expressed and understood.

Downwards the sponsor defines the project's purpose and objectives, provides decisions, resources and directs the project manager. Upwards the sponsor realises the project and its benefits. Laterally the sponsor monitors the project context and provides key communication with stakeholders.

Projects exist in various forms in organisations, and some roles may be described or named differently. Appendix 1 describes examples of such variances that are based on the generic structure illustrated in Figure 3.1.

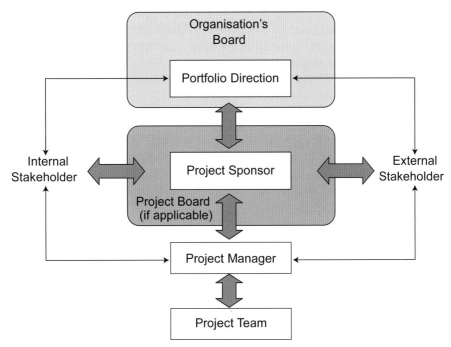

Figure 3.1   Organisational context

4 The attributes for successful sponsorship

The effectiveness of the project sponsor is the best single predictor of project success or failure. Organisations should therefore ensure they always appoint a named sponsor to every project early in its lifecycle.

There are three critical success attributes that project-owning organisations should consider to improve effective sponsorship:
1. **Support:** sponsors should have appropriate organisational support in terms of clear authority, access to decision makers and adequate resources.
2. **Continuity:** there should be continuity of sponsorship through the life cycle, including when necessary appointing a replacement with effective handover between individuals.
3. **Alignment:** sponsors should be motivated to act in the long-term interests of the organisation, providing professional and ethical leadership consistent with its culture and values. Other key sponsor attributes to consider are given below.

To be successful as a sponsor, there are five personal attributes:
1. **Understanding**: the sponsor must understand the role, its significance and the project context.
2. **Competence:** the sponsor must have the knowledge, personal attitudes and skills to fulfil the role.
3. **Credibility:** the sponsor must be accepted by stakeholders as suitable for the role.
4. **Commitment**: the sponsor must give the role the personal time and priority necessary to fulfil its duties and responsibilities.
5. **Engagement:** the sponsor must be willing to take personal ownership of the project and to ensure that effective communications are in place and be able to influence people.

These personal attributes are expanded in the checklist in Appendix 2.

5 What the sponsor does for the board

This component describes the governance responsibilities for which the sponsor is accountable either directly or indirectly to the board. By example and advocacy, sponsors should champion the sponsorship role as a key enabler of corporate governance.

SB01 **Provides leadership on culture and values**
The sponsor ensures that the project is managed in a way that is consistent with the culture and values established from the top of the organisation by its board. The sponsor should create an environment in which decisions made about the project are taken using realistic information on forecasts and progress.

SB02 **Owns the business case**
The sponsor oversees the production and approval of the project business case, ensuring compliance with all related guidelines.
The sponsor should set the success criteria for the project through consultation with the board, key stakeholders and the project manager. Assumptions and constraints should be challenged where necessary to ensure realistic expectations.

SB03 **Keeps project aligned with organisation's strategy and portfolio direction**
The sponsor makes sure that changes in strategic direction by the business are reflected and communicated to project management teams. Such changes must be reflected in the project objectives, business case and documentation such that a consistent view is authorised and maintained. This should include the possibility of recommending the cancellation of the project.

SB04 **Governs project risk**
The sponsor ensures that the organisation's appetite for risk is reflected in the project, and that corporate risk policies and procedures are complied with. The sponsor should ensure that the scope of risk management delegated to the project manager is clearly understood, that risk reviews are carried out regularly and that provision is made for any further contingencies which may have to be handled differently. In doing so, the sponsor should own those risks that they are best placed to influence. Risk management should also include taking a considered view of the impact of the project on stakeholders and its environment. The sponsor should encourage good communication on risk management between the project manager and the rest of the organisation.

SB05 Works with other sponsors

The sponsor proactively supports other sponsors to achieve their business cases in a collaborative fashion, particularly in programme and portfolio management. This should be encouraged by the board. It is particularly important for ensuring that the corporate ethics and culture are not distorted or changed by project teams. It is the sponsor's role to ensure that the project is represented at senior stakeholder forums in order to promote rational and informed decisions about the project. The sponsor can also present decisions made within the project to review forums to promote understanding and agreement with the stakeholders in the senior management community.

SB06 Focuses on realisation of benefits

The sponsor ensures that throughout the project life cycle there is rigour applied to the management of benefits. Benefits should be included in reviews. This will require an understanding of how the benefits will arise, be measured and tracked, and whether any changes in the operational environment might affect them. Typically responsibility for delivering the benefits will be handed over to users once the project is finished, making clear where accountability remains.

SB07 Recommends opportunities to optimise cost/benefits

The sponsor should ensure that project management teams are receptive to change. In particular the sponsor must encourage and support the project manager to optimise the cost-benefit of the project.

SB08 Ensures continuity of sponsorship

Continuity in the sponsorship role should be a prime consideration. If a sponsor is expected to change during the life of the project, then the sponsor should be asked to prepare for the change well in advance. The board should arrange a full handover briefing and confirmation from the new sponsor that the handover has been accepted.

SB09 Provides assurance

The sponsor gives assurance to the board that governance arrangements and policies are being applied. If the project is being managed in phases or stages, which is good practice, then the sponsor authorises progress through gates subject to suitable assurances. The sponsor also gives assurance about project delivery, and should recovery in project performance be required, responds accordingly, whilst keeping the board informed of the implications. In performing these responsibilities the sponsor should invite independent advice and appraisal when appropriate.

SB10 **Provides feedback and lessons learnt**
The sponsor ensures that a learning process is established on the project, feeding lessons learnt into organisational improvement. The sponsor ensures that stakeholders have effective methods of raising their concerns including a mechanism for 'whistle-blowing' that bypasses the project hierarchy and that may, in extreme situations, bypass the sponsor.

6 What the sponsor does for the project manager

This component describes the governance activities between the sponsor and the project manager.

SP01   Provides timely decisions

The sponsor takes the project decisions that the project manager should not be authorised to take, at the time when they are required. If the project manager advises that any of these decisions are problematic or incompatible with other decisions, the sponsor should take the action required to resolve the issues.

SP02   Clarifies decision-making framework

The sponsor should clarify the criteria used to escalate decisions. Too much escalation will undermine the project manager's authority, whilst too little could make the sponsor ineffective. By making decisions and ensuring their implementation, as part of a project board if applicable, the sponsor creates confidence in the project.

SP03   Clarifies business priorities and strategy

The sponsor articulates the context, rationale and objectives of the project, and focuses project management on delivery outcomes. The sponsor must be able to explain the business case, including the high-level costs and anticipated benefits of the project.

SP04   Communicates business issues

The sponsor keeps the project manager informed of matters relating to board and stakeholder decisions which could have an impact on the success of the project and takes responsibility for actions that require senior management commitment.

SP05   Provides resources

The sponsor is required to interpret the requests for resources from the project manager and ensure that reasonable requests are met. This may include approval of funding and purchasing requests. The sponsor should support the project manager in realising appropriate resource requests. This might require building a coalition of stakeholders that will support delivery of the project.

SP06 **Engenders trust**

Sponsors use their influence and status to engender an environment of trust and respect across the organisation. The sponsor should ensure that problems and issues facing the project should be heard constructively and not seen simply as a mechanism to find blame or fault. The project manager must feel confident to report problems without the worry of inappropriate accusation.

SP07 **Manages relationships**

The sponsor personally develops relationships of trust and influence with the most senior and influential stakeholders. The sponsor uses these relationships to communicate the project's vision and benefits, proactively and systematically communicates output from these relationships to the project manager and champions relationship development across the project.

SP08 **Supports the project manager's role**

The sponsor should support the project manager using their wider influence within the organisation. If project recovery action is required, the sponsor should provide appropriate flexibility and support. The sponsor should also review and improve the performance of the project manager. These activities require regular meetings, informed questioning, praise when due, advice and, if necessary, constructive criticism. If necessary, the sponsor should be prepared to replace the project manager.

SP09 **Promotes ethical working**

The sponsor should transmit the culture of the organisation to the project manager and to the wider project team. The transmission of corporate ethics and culture to the project manager and the team must be addressed not only through written documents such as terms of engagement but also reinforced through example and face-to-face briefings.

7 What the sponsor does for other stakeholders

This component describes the governance activities between the sponsor and stakeholders additional to the board and project manager.

Stakeholders potentially comprise a wide range of parties. Clients (on behalf of whom a project may be delivered), users (those who will use or operate project outputs) and supplying organisations (who contribute to project execution or to the operation of the project's outputs) are three key groups. Stakeholders may also include regulators, competitors, pressure groups, financiers, insurers, politicians and others.

SS01   **Engages stakeholders**
The project sponsor should ensure all stakeholders with influence on and/or impacted by the project are identified and their relationship with the project assessed and managed. This could include approval and oversight of the stakeholder management plan. Differences in ethical frameworks between stakeholders should be identified and addressed.

SS02   **Governs stakeholder communications**
The project sponsor should establish appropriate communication mechanisms for each group of stakeholders and ensure these are suitably carried out throughout the life of the project. At a personal level the sponsor should develop relationships of trust and influence with the most senior and influential project stakeholders, using these relationships to communicate the project's vision and benefits, receive feedback and to provide a conduit for escalating where appropriate project issues and concerns between different stakeholders, the board and the project manager.

SS03   **Directs client relationship**
The project sponsor should ensure that the project's governance is compatible with the client's governance requirements. This will include planning the process of making decisions that are required by the client and that have to be taken by the sponsor. It may also involve working to the board and possibly with the client to address issues that are beyond the control of the project manager.

SS04 **Directs governance of users**
The sponsor should ensure appropriate user governance is in place. This includes representation of user needs on governance bodies. This is often achieved by appointing one or more senior users to a project board. A senior user may provide user input to project decisions, facilitate changes required by the users (subject to normal change control), and manage user contributions to the project. Users may be required to contribute to and sign off the project requirements, agree acceptance criteria for the project outputs and verify that outputs delivered by the project are fit for purpose, prior to operational use.

SS05 **Directs governance of suppliers**
The sponsor should ensure appropriate governance is in place for each internal or external supplier. This should include due diligence on any contract, ensuring it reflects all legal (see Appendix 4) and governance requirements, and that the suppliers have the capability to meet the needs of the project in a timely and adequate way. An appropriate formal mechanism for communication with suppliers should be in place and they may be represented on the project board. The sponsor should clarify their role in contract termination decisions, retaining authority for such decisions where there is a need to do so.

SS06 **Arbitrates between stakeholders**
Whilst the majority of decisions regarding the project will be taken by the project manager, there will be occasions when a dispute arises which will be escalated to the sponsor. The type of issues escalated will normally affect the key milestones, deliverables and business benefits. Conflicts may arise between stakeholders during the life of a project. The sponsor should work to avoid or resolve such situations either directly or as the chair of a project board.

Conclusion

In focusing on governance aspects, this guide presents a framework for project sponsorship. It is governance requirements that shape the role. Organisations may add management tasks in particular cases. Similarly, the role might be modified by the adoption of a particular project or programme management methodology. However, the duties presented above cover the essence of the role.

Appendix 1 – Special cases of organisational context

Differentiation between the organisation's board and project boards

Responsibility for an organisation's governance is vested in its board. *Directing Change* (2005) recommends that an organisation's governance should include the governance of project management and identifies project sponsorship to be a key component of this process. Authority to exercise the powers of project sponsorship should therefore be delegated via a path that can be traced to the organisation's board.

Some project management methodologies recommend the use of a project board for the governance of each project. In these circumstances, the project manager is accountable for the project's performance to the project board. Whilst recognising a project board's responsibility, this guide recommends that one member of the project board should be nominated as the project sponsor. This ensures that there is a single path of communication for all decisions associated with the project sponsor's role.

Projects and programmes

In project management terminology, a programme refers to a group of related projects. This guide, like the APM guides to the governance of project management, *Directing Change* (2005) and *Co-directing Change* (2007), uses the word project to refer to both projects and programmes.

This guide recommends that each programme and each of its constituent projects should have a sponsor. These will usually be different people. However there are different possibilities. For example each project may have a different sponsor with delegated authority from the programme manager. In contrast (as shown in Figure A.1) the programme manager could sponsor all of the programme's constituent projects.

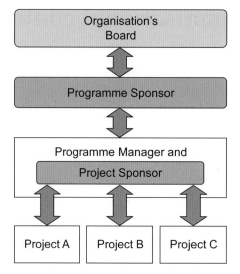

Figure A.1   Programme and project sponsorship

Multi-owned projects

A project is multi-owned if more than one organisation shares ultimate control over the decision-making process that affects fundamental aspects of the project. Fundamental aspects of a project include establishing or modifying the roles of the parties concerned and the project purpose, objectives and scope. Typically, a multi-owned project will be governed by a project board that includes representation from each owning organisation. These representatives are also likely to be the sponsor for the project within their own organisation. However, as with all project boards, and for the same reasons, this guide recommends that one member of such a project board should be nominated as the overall project sponsor.

Multi-organisational projects

Many projects involve more than one organisation, even if the project's ownership is not shared. Examples include projects that involve client–contractor relationships and projects that are reliant on the contribution of more than one stakeholder organisation (see Figure A.2). In these circumstances each organisation may regard its contribution as a project in its own right. Where this is the case, this guide recommends that each organisation should be able to identify the person who fulfils their project sponsor's role. It should be noted that this guide applies to both client and customer organisations.

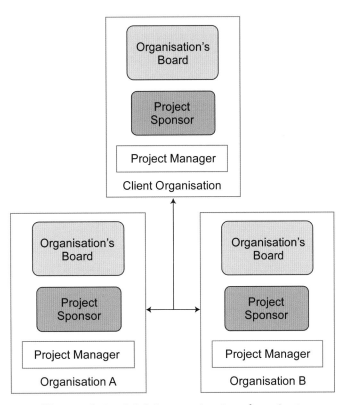

Figure A.2 Multi-organisational projects

Different terminology

In some project management methodologies the relationship between the generic diagram (Figure 3.1) in this guide and the different roles in a particular methodology may need clarification to ensure that the sponsor knows who to work with for each aspect of the role. For example in some methodologies benefits realisation is split from the project manager role and becomes the responsibility of one or more business change managers who also report to the sponsor. This does not alter the relationships shown in figure 3.1 but adds some complexity for the sponsor in discharging the governance responsibilities. See Figure A.3.

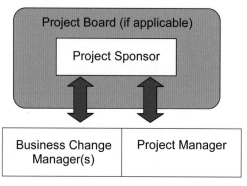

Figure A.3   Different roles

Appendix 2 – Choosing a project sponsor

The organisation should consider three critical success attributes to improve effective sponsorship: organisational support, continuity and alignment of interests. In addition, the following lists expand upon the five personal attributes identified in section 4.

Understanding

☐ Understands the organisation's governance arrangements
☐ Understands the sponsorship role
☐ Understands the project context
☐ Appreciates how the project contributes to the corporate strategy

Competence

☐ Provides clarity of direction
☐ Identifies and focuses on what matters most
☐ Delegates authority to appropriate levels
☐ Manages people and other resources effectively
☐ Makes effective decisions and takes decisive action when necessary
☐ Motivates people
☐ Negotiates effectively
☐ Has relevant experience
☐ Has sufficient appreciation of the project's technical requirements
☐ Has a good understanding of project management
☐ Self-aware about strengths and weaknesses
☐ Demonstrates good judgement

Credibility

☐ Respected by major stakeholders
☐ Ability to influence internal and external stakeholders
☐ Evident track record
☐ Motivated to act in the long-term interest of the organisation

Commitment

☐ Expected time commitment agreed, short and long term

Engagement

☐ Has other responsibilities within the organisation that gives insight into its dynamics
☐ Aligns the project with the interests of the organisation
☐ Obtains regular updates on the organisation's strategy

Appendix 3 – Sponsorship checklists

The checklist below covers the governance responsibilities for which the sponsor is accountable either directly or indirectly to the board.

Ref	Description	Yes	No
SB01	Is the sponsor's leadership consistent with the organisation's culture and values?	☐	☐
SB01	Can be the board be assured that project decisions are taken using realistic information?	☐	☐
SB02	Does the sponsor own the project business case?	☐	☐
SB02	Does the business case comply with the organisation's guidelines?	☐	☐
SB02	Has the control of risk and contingency been agreed?	☐	☐
SB02	Are constraints and assumptions challenged to ensure realistic expectations?	☐	☐
SB03	Does the sponsor have clear authority for this role?	☐	☐
SB03	Are mechanisms in place to ensure that the sponsor is kept informed of changes to the organisation's strategy?	☐	☐
SB03	Does the sponsor keep the project aligned with the organisation's strategy?	☐	☐
SB03	Would the project be closed when appropriate?	☐	☐
SB04	Are the escalation and resolution processes appropriate?	☐	☐
SB04	Does the sponsor assure that the project risk profile is commensurate with the organisation's risk appetite?	☐	☐
SB04	Are there clear lines of communication with the rest of the organisation for discussing risks?	☐	☐
SB04	Does the sponsor own those risks that they are best placed to influence?	☐	☐
SB04	Are corporate risk policies and procedures complied with?	☐	☐
SB05	Is there a forum for meeting other sponsors?	☐	☐
SB06	Is the business case maintained and reviewed to ensure it is valid and achievable?	☐	☐
SB06	Has the sponsor agreed responsibilities for effective benefit realisation?	☐	☐
SB06	Has the sponsor agreed appropriate mechanisms for control over benefit realisation efforts including integration with plans and budgets?	☐	☐
SB06	Is progress towards benefit realisation being actively maintained and reported?	☐	☐

Ref	Description	Yes	No
SB07	Does the sponsor motivate the project manager to optimise the cost–benefits?	☐	☐
SB07	Does the sponsor identify opportunities beyond the original business case?	☐	☐
SB08	Is the sponsor's role continuous over the full life cycle of the project?	☐	☐
SB08	Is there agreement about who decides and arranges a change of sponsor?	☐	☐
SB08	Should a 'shadow' sponsor be in place to ensure continuity in case of a change of sponsor?	☐	☐
SB09	Does the sponsor assure that governance arrangements are applied?	☐	☐
SB09	Does the sponsor assure that corporate policies are applied?	☐	☐
SB09	Does the sponsor assure that reported commitment and expenditure forecasts are realistic?	☐	☐
SB09	Does the sponsor assure that milestone forecasts are realistic?	☐	☐
SB09	Does the sponsor assure that the forecasted performance of project deliverables is realistic?	☐	☐
SB09	Does the sponsor seek independent advice and appraisal when appropriate?	☐	☐
SB10	Does the sponsor ensure that processes are in place such that experience of project success and failure is shared across the wider organisation?	☐	☐
SB10	Is there a 'speak-up' or 'whistle-blowing' line available?	☐	☐

The checklist below covers the governance activities between the sponsor and the project manager.

Ref	Description	Yes	No
SP01	Does the project manager know which decisions will be taken by the sponsor and when?	☐	☐
SP01	Have the sponsor's decisions been accepted by the project manager as being a sound basis on which to proceed?	☐	☐
SP02	Have escalation criteria for risks and issues been agreed?	☐	☐
SP02	Does the project manager escalate risks and issues to the sponsor in good time?	☐	☐
SP02	Has risk and contingency been allocated between the sponsor and the project manager?	☐	☐
SP03	Have the project's purpose and objectives been adequately defined?	☐	☐

Sponsoring Change

Ref	Description	Yes	No
SP03	Does the project manager understand the project's benefits and business case?	☐	☐
SP03	Does the project manager understand the project in the context of the organisation's strategy?	☐	☐
SP04	Is there a structure to provide good communication between the sponsor and the project manager?	☐	☐
SP05	Does the sponsor ensure provision of financial and other resources as required by the project?	☐	☐
SP06	Does the sponsor encourage open and honest reporting?	☐	☐
SP07	Does the sponsor's handling of stakeholder relationships help the project manager to fulfil their role?	☐	☐
SP08	Does the sponsor respond constructively to issues identified by the project?	☐	☐
SP08	Is there a forum for the project sponsor to review the project manager's performance and does it promote improvement?	☐	☐
SP08	Is the sponsor satisfied that the project is managed by a suitable project manager?	☐	☐
SP08	Does the sponsor support the project management methods used by the project manager and any support office?	☐	☐
SP08	If project recovery needs to be sponsored, does the sponsor give the project appropriate flexibility and support?	☐	☐
SP09	Does the sponsor, both by policy and by example, convey the organisation's corporate culture and ethics to the project?	☐	☐

The checklist below covers the governance activities between the sponsor and stakeholders additional to the board.

Ref	Description	Yes	No
SS01	Have significant stakeholders been identified?	☐	☐
SS01	Is the influence of each understood within the context of the whole stakeholder community?	☐	☐
SS01	Has their relationship with the project been assessed?	☐	☐
SS01	Does the sponsor oversee an approved stakeholder management plan?	☐	☐
SS01	Are differences in ethical frameworks identified and addressed?	☐	☐
SS02	Have stakeholder communication needs been built into the project plan?	☐	☐
SS02	Does the sponsor relate to key stakeholders?	☐	☐
SS03	Have the implications of the client's governance process been built in to the project's governance?	☐	☐
SS03	Does the sponsor plan to make those decisions that are required by the client and that the sponsor has to take?	☐	☐

Ref	Description	Yes	No
SS03	Does the sponsor provide an effective means of resolving client issues that cannot be resolved by the project manager?	☐	☐
SS03	Does the sponsor expedite their organisation's issues with the client when such intervention is warranted?	☐	☐
SS03	Does the sponsor exploit the project to develop longer term strategic relationships with the client's organisation?	☐	☐
SS04	Has appropriate user representation been built into the project management structure?	☐	☐
SS04	Does the project communications strategy include provision for effective input by users, particularly in terms of requirements, and development and operational needs?	☐	☐
SS04	Is provision made for active user involvement, which allows for changes to be made as necessary and through the appropriate channels?	☐	☐
SS04	Are users appropriately involved in the project decision-making and problem-resolution processes?	☐	☐
SS04	Have user representatives agreed the project acceptance criteria?	☐	☐
SS04	Does the project plan incorporate appropriate user readiness activities such as training and acceptance testing prior to handover for operational use?	☐	☐
SS05	Have governance implications of internal supplies been identified and resolved?	☐	☐
SS05	Does due diligence before contract commitment reflect legal and governance requirements?	☐	☐
SS05	Have due diligence processes been carried out to verify the capability and commitment of each supplier with respect to the project?	☐	☐
SS05	Has a structure been put in place for formal communications between each supplier and appropriate project representatives?	☐	☐
SS05	Has provision been made for the project sponsor to meet with supplier's senior management if and when contract reviews are required?	☐	☐
SS05	Does the sponsor have authority to participate in multi-contract project strategy reviews?	☐	☐
SS05	Will the sponsor have suitable input on any decision to terminate a contract?	☐	☐
SS06	Is there a forum or process enabling potential stakeholder conflicts to be identified and avoided?	☐	☐
SS06	Is there provision for escalating disputes between stakeholders to the sponsor for resolution?	☐	☐
SS06	Does the sponsor protect the success criteria for the project in resolving stakeholder conflicts?	☐	☐

Appendix 4 – Legal aspects

Based on an interpretation of English law

The organisation

should:
- clarify the extent of the sponsor's liabilities e.g. as a director.
- distinguish between matters and expenditure levels for which the sponsor is authorised and 'matters reserved for the board'.
- authorise to enter into project-relevant contracts on behalf of the organisation and to negotiate, arbitrate or litigate.
- ensure that the extent and limits of the sponsor's authority are clearly delineated to insiders and outsiders.
- ensure that sponsors are covered under their organisation's D&O (directors and officers) insurance if appropriate given their responsibilities and potential liabilities.

The sponsor

should check that effective systems ensure compliance with regulatory requirements and internal policies, in particular that:
- any company set up in respect of the project, or to receive funds due to and from the project has an appropriate corporate form and is keeping financial and other records as required by the relevant regulator.
- any company set up in respect of the project is operating with such levels of compliance, transparency and integrity that there can be no perception by the authorities that it offers a vehicle for laundering the proceeds of crime.
- any intellectual property created in the course of the activities of the project has been appropriately protected in law so as to minimise opportunities for unlawful exploitation by other parties.
- the services of workers on the project are being retained in compliance with applicable employment legislation.
- the activities of the project are being conducted in such a way as to comply with applicable Data Protection, Health, Safety and Environmental legislation.
- the activities of the project involving co-operation with other similar businesses are conducted in such a way as not to be perceived by the authorities as constituting unfair competition.
- in a situation of potential insolvency, the project can be closed promptly and that the activities involved in its closure cannot be construed by the authorities as constituting or contributing to wrongful or fraudulent trading.
- the multi-jurisdictional compliance aspects are considered.

Appendix 5 – Bibliography

American National Standards Institute (2008) *ANSI/PMI–99–001–2008: A Guide to the Project Manager Body of Knowledge*, PMBOK® Guide, 4th edition, Project Management Institute Inc.

Association for Project Management (2005), *Directing Change: A Guide to the Governance of Project Management*, APM Publishing.

Association for Project Management (2006), *APM Body of Knowledge*, 5th edition, APM Publishing.

Association for Project Management (2007), *Co-Directing Change: A Guide to the Governance of Multi-Owned Projects*, APM Publishing.

British Standard BS6079–1:2002, *Project Management*, *Part 1: Guide to Project Management*, British Standards Institution.

UK Office of Government Commerce (OGC) (2007), *Managing Successful Programmes*, The Stationery Office.